About Skill Builders
Math
Grade 3

Welcome to Skill Builders *Math* for third grade. This book is designed to improve children's math skills through focused practice. This full-color workbook contains grade-level-appropriate activities based on national standards to help ensure that children master basic skills before progressing.

More than 70 pages of activities cover essential math skills such as addition and subtraction, multiplication and division, and data analysis. The book's colorful, inviting format, easy-to-follow directions, and clear examples help build children's confidence and make math more accessible and enjoyable.

The Skill Builders series offers workbooks that are perfect for keeping skills sharp during the school year or preparing students for the next grade.

Credits:

Content Editor: Alan Hull
Copy Editor: Beatrice Allen
Layout and Cover Design: Nick Greenwood

carsondellosa.com
Carson-Dellosa Publishing LLC
Greensboro, North Carolina

ISBN 978-1-936023-25-7
07-152151151

Table of Contents

Addition and Subtraction Facts to 20

Solve each problem.

1. $2 + 3 = $ _5_

2. $1 + 9 = $ _10_

3. $5 + 2 = $ _7_

4. $15 - 5 = $ _10_

5. $16 - 7 = $ _9_

6. $10 - 5 = $ _5_

7. $9 + 2 = $ _11_

8. $13 + 6 = $ _7_

9. $11 - 6 = $ _5_

10. $9 - 3 = $ _6_

11. $10 + 7 = $ _17_

12. $10 + 3 = $ _13_

13. $9 - 9 = $ _0_

14. $9 + 3 = $ _12_

15. $12 - 4 = $ _8_

16. $6 + 6 = $ _12_

17. $7 - 4 = $ _3_

18. $8 + 7 = $ _15_

19. $15 - 6 = $ _9_

20. $9 + 6 = $ _15_

21. $11 - 4 = $ _7_

22. $14 - 7 = $ _7_

23. $8 + 4 = $ _12_

24. $13 - 9 = $ _4_

25. $7 + 2 = $ _9_

26. $6 + 8 = $ _14_

Addition and Subtraction Facts to 20

Solve each problem.

1. $\begin{array}{r} 16 \\ -\ 6 \\ \hline \end{array}$

2. $\begin{array}{r} 10 \\ -\ 0 \\ \hline 10 \end{array}$

3. $\begin{array}{r} 4 \\ +\ 9 \\ \hline \end{array}$

4. $\begin{array}{r} 9 \\ +\ 1 \\ \hline 10 \end{array}$

5. $\begin{array}{r} 5 \\ +\ 8 \\ \hline \end{array}$

6. $\begin{array}{r} 3 \\ +\ 7 \\ \hline 10 \end{array}$

7. $\begin{array}{r} 18 \\ -\ 9 \\ \hline \end{array}$

8. $\begin{array}{r} 9 \\ +\ 5 \\ \hline 14 \end{array}$

9. $\begin{array}{r} 16 \\ -\ 7 \\ \hline \end{array}$

10. $\begin{array}{r} 8 \\ -\ 1 \\ \hline 7 \end{array}$

11. $\begin{array}{r} 7 \\ -\ 0 \\ \hline \end{array}$

12. $\begin{array}{r} 5 \\ +\ 4 \\ \hline 9 \end{array}$

13. $\begin{array}{r} 7 \\ +\ 6 \\ \hline 13 \end{array}$

14. $\begin{array}{r} 14 \\ -\ 9 \\ \hline \end{array}$

15. $\begin{array}{r} 10 \\ -\ 4 \\ \hline \end{array}$

16. $\begin{array}{r} 11 \\ -\ 3 \\ \hline \end{array}$

17. $\begin{array}{r} 8 \\ +\ 8 \\ \hline \end{array}$

18. $\begin{array}{r} 16 \\ -\ 9 \\ \hline \end{array}$

19. $\begin{array}{r} 14 \\ -\ 5 \\ \hline \end{array}$

20. $\begin{array}{r} 7 \\ +\ 8 \\ \hline \end{array}$

Column Addition

Solve each problem.

When adding three numbers, look for a fact or facts that you already know and add those numbers. Then, add the third number to the sum.

$$\begin{array}{r} 7 \\ 3 \\ +5 \\ \hline 15 \end{array} \Big\rangle 10 \qquad \begin{array}{r} \\ \\ +5 \\ \hline 15 \end{array}$$

Add 7 + 3 = 10.
Then, add 10 + 5 = 15.

1.
$$\begin{array}{r} 2 \\ 8 \\ +\ 3 \\ \hline \end{array}$$

2.
$$\begin{array}{r} 6 \\ 4 \\ +\ 3 \\ \hline \end{array}$$

3.
$$\begin{array}{r} 4 \\ 4 \\ +\ 3 \\ \hline \end{array}$$

4.
$$\begin{array}{r} 5 \\ 5 \\ +\ 5 \\ \hline \end{array}$$

5.
$$\begin{array}{r} 7 \\ 7 \\ +\ 3 \\ \hline \end{array}$$

6.
$$\begin{array}{r} 5 \\ 3 \\ 4 \\ +\ 1 \\ \hline \end{array}$$

7.
$$\begin{array}{r} 4 \\ 8 \\ 2 \\ +\ 1 \\ \hline \end{array}$$

8.
$$\begin{array}{r} 2 \\ 9 \\ 1 \\ +\ 3 \\ \hline \end{array}$$

9.
$$\begin{array}{r} 7 \\ 5 \\ 3 \\ +\ 3 \\ \hline \end{array}$$

10.
$$\begin{array}{r} 8 \\ 2 \\ 5 \\ +\ 3 \\ \hline \end{array}$$

11.
$$\begin{array}{r} 3 \\ 7 \\ 5 \\ +\ 1 \\ \hline \end{array}$$

12.
$$\begin{array}{r} 4 \\ 8 \\ 2 \\ +\ 3 \\ \hline \end{array}$$

13.
$$\begin{array}{r} 9 \\ 1 \\ 5 \\ +\ 2 \\ \hline \end{array}$$

14.
$$\begin{array}{r} 6 \\ 6 \\ 3 \\ +\ 3 \\ \hline \end{array}$$

15.
$$\begin{array}{r} 7 \\ 8 \\ 1 \\ +\ 2 \\ \hline \end{array}$$

Odd and Even Numbers

Color the even numbers between 0 and 51 blue.
Color the odd numbers between 0 and 51 green.
Color the even numbers between 52 and 100 orange.
Color the odd numbers between 52 and 100 yellow.

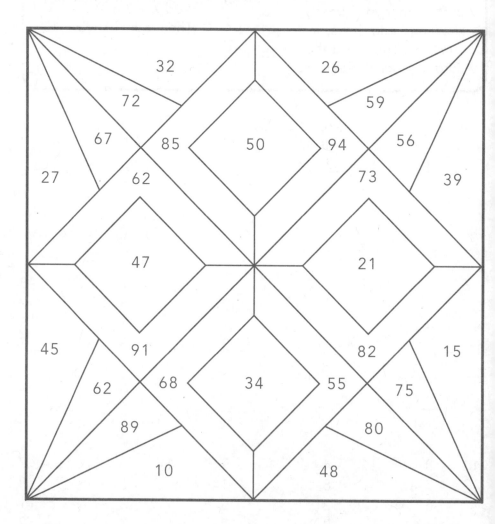

Addition without Regrouping

Solve each problem.

To add three-digit numbers, follow these steps.

1. Add the ones.   2. Add the tens.   3. Add the hundreds.

```
  4 2 7              4 2 7                4 2 7
+ 3 3 1            + 3 3 1            +   3 3 1
      8                5 8              7 5 8
```

1.   64
    + 25

2.   47
    + 31

3.   13
    + 45

4.   55
    + 30

5.   52
    + 37

6.   36
    + 23

7.   15
    + 72

8.   18
    + 81

9.   84
    + 12

10.   352
    + 436

11.   475
    + 510

12.   724
    + 143

13.   650
    + 227

14.   298
    + 500

15.   525
    + 261

16.   632
    + 155

Subtraction without Regrouping

Solve each problem.

1. Subtract the ones.	2. Subtract the tens.	3. Subtract the hundreds.
5 6 **4** − 1 3 **2** **2**	5 **6** 4 − 1 **3** 2 **3** 2	**5** 6 4 − **1** 3 2 **4** 3 2

1. 86
   − 32

2. 52
   − 12

3. 67
   − 45

4. 95
   − 30

5. 38
   − 14

6. 75
   − 52

7. 88
   − 37

8. 74
   − 24

9. 57
   − 33

10. 49
    − 25

11. 36
    − 14

12. 87
    − 77

13. 283
   − 220

14. 488
   − 351

15. 695
   − 233

16. 348
   − 33

Addition with Regrouping

Solve each problem.

1. Add the ones.
   Regroup 13 ones
   as 1 ten, 3 ones.

```
  1
3 7 5
+ 2 6 8
      3
```

2. Add the tens.
   Regroup 14 tens
   as 1 hundred, 4 tens.

```
1 1
3 7 5
+ 2 6 8
  4 3
```

3. Add the
   hundreds.

```
1 1
3 7 5
+ 2 6 8
6 4 3
```

1. 27
  + 24

2. 39
  + 53

3. 46
  + 37

4. 57
  + 29

5. 75
  + 19

6. 93
  + 7

7. 58
  + 34

8. 64
  + 28

9. 66
  + 27

10. 79
   + 32

11. 43
   + 27

12. 56
   + 58

13. 693
   + 127

14. 486
   + 236

15. 567
   + 169

16. 583
   + 237

Subtraction with Regrouping

Solve each problem.

1. Subtract the ones. You cannot subtract 6 from 4. Regroup 3 tens as 2 tens, 10 ones.

$$\begin{array}{r} 5\ \overset{2}{\cancel{3}}\ \overset{14}{4} \\ -\ 2\ 5\ 6 \\ \hline 8 \end{array}$$

2. Subtract the tens. You cannot subtract 5 tens from 2 tens. Regroup 5 hundreds as 4 hundreds, 10 tens.

$$\begin{array}{r} \overset{4}{\cancel{5}}\ \overset{\overset{12}{\cancel{2}}}{}\ \overset{14}{4} \\ -\ 2\ 5\ 6 \\ \hline 7\ 8 \end{array}$$

3. Subtract the hundreds.

$$\begin{array}{r} \overset{4}{\cancel{5}}\ \overset{\overset{12}{2}}{}\ \overset{14}{4} \\ -\ 2\ 5\ 6 \\ \hline 2\ 7\ 8 \end{array}$$

1. $\begin{array}{r} 36 \\ -\ 17 \\ \hline \end{array}$

2. $\begin{array}{r} 98 \\ -\ 19 \\ \hline \end{array}$

3. $\begin{array}{r} 28 \\ -\ 9 \\ \hline \end{array}$

4. $\begin{array}{r} 41 \\ -\ 15 \\ \hline \end{array}$

5. $\begin{array}{r} 72 \\ -\ 53 \\ \hline \end{array}$

6. $\begin{array}{r} 85 \\ -\ 27 \\ \hline \end{array}$

7. $\begin{array}{r} 43 \\ -\ 29 \\ \hline \end{array}$

8. $\begin{array}{r} 96 \\ -\ 37 \\ \hline \end{array}$

9. $\begin{array}{r} 47 \\ -\ 19 \\ \hline \end{array}$

10. $\begin{array}{r} 94 \\ -\ 26 \\ \hline \end{array}$

11. $\begin{array}{r} 75 \\ -\ 39 \\ \hline \end{array}$

12. $\begin{array}{r} 61 \\ -\ 22 \\ \hline \end{array}$

13. $\begin{array}{r} 767 \\ -\ 18 \\ \hline \end{array}$

14. $\begin{array}{r} 350 \\ -\ 68 \\ \hline \end{array}$

15. $\begin{array}{r} 482 \\ -\ 95 \\ \hline \end{array}$

16. $\begin{array}{r} 465 \\ -\ 187 \\ \hline \end{array}$

Addition and Subtraction
Problem Solving

Solve each problem. Show your work. Then, write the answer on the line.

1. Sam's basketball team scored 42 points. Nick's team only scored 28 points.

   How many more points did Sam's team score than Nick's team?

   _____

2. Jan had 57 seashells in her collection. Her aunt sent her 26 more.

   How many seashells does Jan have now?

   _____

3. Nathan had 82 toy cars. He saved 15 special cars and gave the rest to his cousin.

   How many cars did he give to his cousin?

   _____

4. A bike shop had 43 adult bikes and 38 children's bikes.

   How many bikes does the shop have altogether?

   _____

Addition and Subtraction
Problem Solving

Solve each problem. Show your work. Then, write the answer on the line.

1. Roberto had 346 trading cards. He sold 188 cards at a trading card show.

   How many cards does he have left?

   _____

2. Mindy's class saved 121 soup labels. The rest of the school saved 699 labels.

   How many labels does the school have altogether?

   _____

3. Trey had 623 rocks in his collection. He found 17 more when he went hiking last week.

   How many rocks does Trey have in all?

   _____

4. The pet store had 435 fish for sale. It sold 178 fish last week.

   How many fish does the store have left?

   _____

Place Value

Write how many tens and ones are in each picture and how many there are in total.

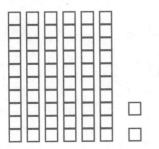

1.

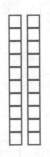

___6___ tens ___2___ ones

total ___62___

_____ tens _____ ones

total _____

2.

_____ ten _____ ones

total _____

3.

_____ tens _____ ones

total _____

Place Value

Write how many hundreds, tens, and ones are in each picture and how many there are in total.

1.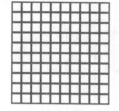

_____ hundreds + _____ tens + _____ ones = _____

2.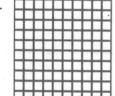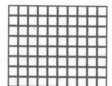

_____ hundreds + _____ tens + _____ ones = _____

3.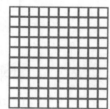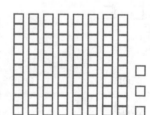

_____ hundreds + _____ tens + _____ ones = _____

Place Value

Write the digits of each number under the correct place value headings.

	Ten Thousands	Thousands	Hundreds	Tens	Ones
5,739	0	5	7	3	9
1. 14,650					
2. 81					
3. 40,736					
4. 1,475					
5. 55,837					
6. 86,902					
7. 4,560					
8. 31,048					
9. 111					
10. 79,277					
11. 93					
12. 99,999					
13. 5					

Place Value

Write the place value of each circled digit.

3,④5 6   **<u>hundreds</u>**   1.   9 0,②8 6 _____

2.   ⑦,3 9 4 _____   3.   ④7,5 1 9 _____

4.   ①6,3 2 1 _____   5.   3 8,1②7 _____

6.   2 5,0④7 _____   7.   ⑧4,0 3 1 _____

8.   3 9,⑤8 6 _____   9.   7②,7 9 7 _____

10.   5 8,7 2⑨ _____   11.   5 9,3⑥8 _____

12.   4 0,3⑦0 _____   13.   3 0,5 8④ _____

14.   ⑦2,5 3 2 _____   15.   8⑥,3 9 5 _____

16.   9⑥,4 1 1 _____   17.   3 9,⑤8 6 _____

18.   8 3,0⑨5 _____   19.   5⓪,8 5 4 _____

Place Value

Write each number in standard form.

$30,000 + 1,000 + 500 + 30 + 3 =$ **31,533**

1. $70,000 + 5,000 + 900 + 40 + 7 =$ _____

2. $90,000 + 3,000 + 700 + 50 + 5 =$ _____

3. $100,000 + 50,000 + 7,000 + 400 + 70 + 9 =$ _____

4. $500,000 + 60,000 + 9,000 + 100 + 20 + 1 =$ _____

5. $300,000 + 40,000 + 300 + 10 + 2 =$ _____

6. $200,000 + 50,000 + 3,000 + 500 + 6 =$ _____

7. $700,000 + 10,000 + 6,000 + 90 + 8 =$ _____

8. $600,000 + 20,000 + 8,000 + 200 + 1 =$ _____

9. $900,000 + 20,000 + 6,000 + 30 + 5 =$ _____

10. $100,000 + 40,000 + 7,000 + 400 + 30 =$ _____

11. $600,000 + 70,000 + 1,000 + 300 + 50 + 6 =$ _____

Place Value

Use the numbers on the houses below to write the correct three- and four-digit numbers.

Three-digit numbers greater than 400

__418__   __481__   __814__   __841__

1. Three-digit numbers less than 500

    _____   _____   _____   _____

2. Three-digit numbers greater than 800

    _____   _____

3. Three-digit numbers greater than 160 and less than 500

    _____   _____   _____

4. Three-digit numbers greater than 450 and less than 820

    _____   _____

5. Four-digit numbers greater than 4,000 and less than 5,400

    _____   _____   _____   _____

6. Four-digit numbers greater than 5,400 and less than 7,000

    _____   _____   _____   _____

7. Four-digit numbers greater than 4,500 and less than 5,000

    _____   _____   _____   _____

8. Four-digit numbers greater than 3,500 and less than 4,000

    _____   _____   _____   _____

Number Maze

Follow the numbers in order from greatest to least. Not every number will be used.

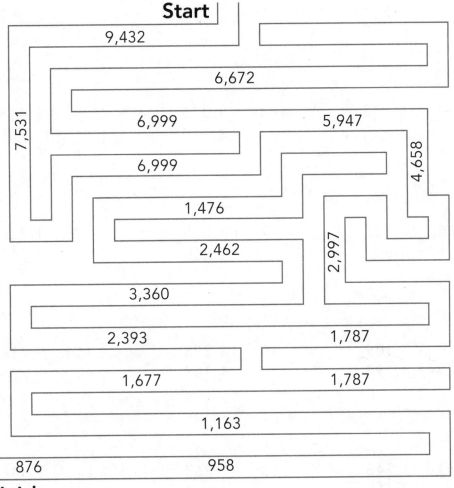

Start

9,432

6,672

6,999   5,947

6,999

7,531

4,658

1,476

2,462

2,997

3,360

2,393   1,787

1,677   1,787

1,163

876   958

Finish

Addition with Regrouping

Solve each problem.

$$
\begin{array}{r}
\overset{1\ 1}{3,261} \\
+\ 5,239 \\
\hline
\mathbf{8,500}
\end{array}
$$

1.
$$
\begin{array}{r}
4,639 \\
+\ 2,073 \\
\hline
\end{array}
$$

2.
$$
\begin{array}{r}
7,216 \\
+\ 2,593 \\
\hline
\end{array}
$$

3.
$$
\begin{array}{r}
2,773 \\
+\ 3,535 \\
\hline
\end{array}
$$

4.
$$
\begin{array}{r}
5,076 \\
+\ 3,970 \\
\hline
\end{array}
$$

5.
$$
\begin{array}{r}
6,415 \\
+\ 1,765 \\
\hline
\end{array}
$$

6.
$$
\begin{array}{r}
3,257 \\
+\ 4,809 \\
\hline
\end{array}
$$

7.
$$
\begin{array}{r}
4,935 \\
+\ 1,260 \\
\hline
\end{array}
$$

8.
$$
\begin{array}{r}
1,224 \\
+\ 3,967 \\
\hline
\end{array}
$$

9.
$$
\begin{array}{r}
2,309 \\
+\ 4,597 \\
\hline
\end{array}
$$

10.
$$
\begin{array}{r}
3,295 \\
+\ 4,305 \\
\hline
\end{array}
$$

11.
$$
\begin{array}{r}
5,716 \\
+\ 1,708 \\
\hline
\end{array}
$$

12.
$$
\begin{array}{r}
1,943 \\
+\ 3,065 \\
\hline
\end{array}
$$

13.
$$
\begin{array}{r}
1,967 \\
+\ 7,120 \\
\hline
\end{array}
$$

14.
$$
\begin{array}{r}
3,846 \\
+\ 2,195 \\
\hline
\end{array}
$$

Subtraction with Regrouping

Solve each problem.

$$\begin{array}{r} {}^{8\ 1\ 6\ 1} \\ \cancel{9},3\cancel{7}5 \\ -\ 4,969 \\ \hline \mathbf{4,406} \end{array}$$

1. 2,772
   − 1,476

2. 3,943
   − 1,876

3. 7,403
   − 2,675

4. 9,800
   − 3,765

5. 5,639
   − 1,879

6. 8,207
   − 4,648

7. 9,730
   − 4,698

8. 7,796
   − 2,994

9. 7,436
   − 5,527

10. 5,943
    − 3,880

11. 3,845
    − 1,966

12. 7,571
    − 3,875

13. 5,965
    − 1,879

14. 4,739
    − 3,465

Addition and Subtraction
Problem Solving

Solve each problem. Show your work. Then, write the answer on the line.

1. On Friday night, 2,479 people went to the concert.
   On Saturday night, 3,210 people went to the concert.

a. How many people went to the two concerts altogether?

b. How many more people attended on Saturday night than on Friday night?

_____

_____

2. East High School had 1,324 graduates.
   West High School had 1,129 graduates.

a. How many students graduated from the two high schools?

b. How many more students graduated from East than from West?

_____

_____

Telling Time: Clock Hands

For problems 1–3, write the time shown on the clocks. For problems 4–7, draw hands on the clocks to show the time.

6 : **50**

1.

_____ : _____

2.

_____ : _____

3.

_____ : _____

4.

12:23

5.

10:25

6.

11:08

7.

4:47

Telling Time: Application

Use the clocks to answer the questions.

1. What time does the clock show? _____

   What time would it be
   if it was 20 minutes earlier? _____

   What time will it be in
   3 hours and 35 minutes? _____

   What time will it be in 65 minutes? _____

2. What time does the clock show? _____

   What time would it be if it
   was 40 minutes earlier? _____

   What time will it be in
   5 hours and 20 minutes? _____

   What time will it be in 50 minutes? _____

3. What time does the clock show? _____

   What time would it be if it was
   4 hours and 15 minutes earlier? _____

   What time will it be in
   2 hours and 15 minutes? _____

   What time will it be in 75 minutes? _____

Multiplication: Comparing Sets

Solve each problem. Use the pictures to create sets.

$2 \times 3 = 6$ or $3 \times 2 = 6$

1. ___ × ___ = ___   or   ___ × ___ = ___

2. ___ × ___ = ___   or   ___ × ___ = ___

3. ___ × ___ = ___   or   ___ × ___ = ___

4. ___ × ___ = ___   or   ___ × ___ = ___

Multiplication: Fact Sequences

Complete each fact sequence.

1. $2 \times 4 = 8$ $3 \times 4 =$ _____ $4 \times 4 =$ _____

2. $5 \times 3 = 15$ $6 \times 3 =$ _____ $7 \times 3 =$ _____

3. $1 \times 6 = 6$ $2 \times 6 =$ _____ $3 \times 6 =$ _____

4. $2 \times 5 = 10$ $3 \times 5 =$ _____ $4 \times 5 =$ _____

5. $3 \times 7 = 21$ $4 \times 7 =$ _____ $5 \times 7 =$ _____

6. $3 \times 4 = 12$ $4 \times 4 =$ _____ $5 \times 4 =$ _____

7. $2 \times 9 = 18$ $3 \times 9 =$ _____ $4 \times 9 =$ _____

8. $4 \times 6 = 24$ $5 \times 6 =$ _____ $6 \times 6 =$ _____

9. $1 \times 8 = 8$ $2 \times 8 =$ _____ $3 \times 8 =$ _____

Multiplication Facts: 3, 4, 5, and 6

Solve each problem.

1. 3 × 1 = _____
   3 × 2 = _____
   3 × 3 = _____
   3 × 4 = _____
   3 × 5 = _____
   3 × 6 = _____
   3 × 7 = _____
   3 × 8 = _____
   3 × 9 = _____
   3 × 10 = _____

2. 4 × 1 = _____
   4 × 2 = _____
   4 × 3 = _____
   4 × 4 = _____
   4 × 5 = _____
   4 × 6 = _____
   4 × 7 = _____
   4 × 8 = _____
   4 × 9 = _____
   4 × 10 = _____

3. 5 × 1 = _____
   5 × 2 = _____
   5 × 3 = _____
   5 × 4 = _____
   5 × 5 = _____
   5 × 6 = _____
   5 × 7 = _____
   5 × 8 = _____
   5 × 9 = _____
   5 × 10 = _____

4. 6 × 1 = _____
   6 × 2 = _____
   6 × 3 = _____
   6 × 4 = _____
   6 × 5 = _____
   6 × 6 = _____
   6 × 7 = _____
   6 × 8 = _____
   6 × 9 = _____
   6 × 10 = _____

Multiplication: Comparing Expressions

Use >, <, or = to describe the relationship between the expressions.

2×6 ⊘< 7×2 1. 5×3 ◯ 4×4

2. 2×4 ◯ 6×1 3. 9×4 ◯ 6×6

4. 7×5 ◯ 6×7 5. 4×5 ◯ 5×3

6. 9×5 ◯ 10×4 7. 6×7 ◯ 7×6

8. 8×4 ◯ 9×3 9. 3×6 ◯ 4×5

10. 3×7 ◯ 5×5 11. 10×5 ◯ 9×7

12. 6×0 ◯ 0×10 13. 2×6 ◯ 3×4

14. 5×4 ◯ 5×3 15. 9×1 ◯ 8×2

16. 7×1 ◯ 6×9 17. 2×10 ◯ 5×4

18. 5×0 ◯ 5×10 19. 5×9 ◯ 4×10

Multiplication Problem Solving

Solve each problem. Show your work. Then, write the answer on the line.

1. Randy had 6 bags. He put 9 marbles in each bag.

   How many marbles did he have?

   _____

2. Stan has 4 stacks of cards with 8 cards in each stack.

   How many cards does he have altogether?

   _____

3. Jennifer jumped over 5 rocks. She jumped over each rock 9 times.

   How many times did she jump?

   _____

4. The skaters skated in 7 groups with 4 in each group.

   How many skaters were there in all?

   _____

Multiplication: Missing Numbers

Write the number to make a true fact.

$9 \times \underline{\textbf{1}} = 9$

1. $3 \times \underline{\hspace{1cm}} = 21$

2. $4 \times \underline{\hspace{1cm}} = 28$

3. $2 \times \underline{\hspace{1cm}} = 16$

4. $5 \times \underline{\hspace{1cm}} = 40$

5. $7 \times \underline{\hspace{1cm}} = 42$

6. $\underline{\hspace{1cm}} \times 4 = 36$

7. $\underline{\hspace{1cm}} \times 6 = 54$

8. $\underline{\hspace{1cm}} \times 8 = 48$

9. $\underline{\hspace{1cm}} \times 3 = 15$

10. $5 \times 4 = \underline{\hspace{1cm}}$

11. $6 \times 2 = \underline{\hspace{1cm}}$

12. $0 \times 5 = \underline{\hspace{1cm}}$

13. $\underline{\hspace{1cm}} \times 7 = 28$

14. $\underline{\hspace{1cm}} \times 2 = 14$

15. $8 \times \underline{\hspace{1cm}} = 56$

16. $8 \times \underline{\hspace{1cm}} = 32$

17. $1 \times \underline{\hspace{1cm}} = 5$

18. $10 \times \underline{\hspace{1cm}} = 0$

19. $\underline{\hspace{1cm}} \times 7 = 49$

20. $\underline{\hspace{1cm}} \times 5 = 50$

21. $9 \times 1 = \underline{\hspace{1cm}}$

22. $6 \times \underline{\hspace{1cm}} = 30$

23. $\underline{\hspace{1cm}} \times 10 = 100$

Multiplication Wheels

Complete each wheel. Multiply from the center number to the edge.

1.

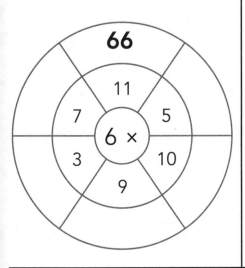

2.

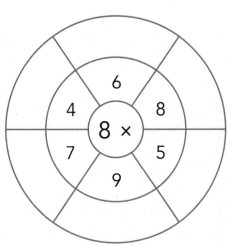

3.

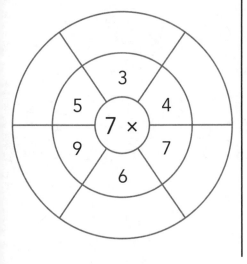

4.

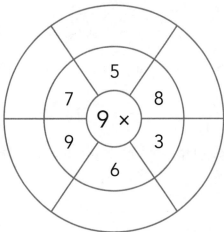

Division Facts

Solve each problem.

How many 4s are there in 8?   __2__ $8 \div 4 =$ __2__

1. How many 6s are there in 18?   _____ $18 \div 6 =$ _____

2. How many 2s are there in 10?   _____ $10 \div 2 =$ _____

3. How many 7s are there in 21?   _____ $21 \div 7 =$ _____

4. How many 5s are there in 20?   _____ $20 \div 5 =$ _____

5. How many 3s are there in 12?   _____ $12 \div 3 =$ _____

6. How many 9s are there in 18?   _____ $18 \div 9 =$ _____

7. How many 1s are there in 7?   _____ $7 \div 1 =$ _____

Division: Matching Facts and Sets

Write the answer for each fact. Draw a line to match the fact with the set.

$16 \div 8 = \underline{2}$

A.

1. $24 \div 4 = \underline{}$

B.

2. $21 \div 3 = \underline{}$

C.

3. $40 \div 8 = \underline{}$

D.

4. $32 \div 4 = \underline{}$

E.

5. $12 \div 4 = \underline{}$

F.

6. $36 \div 4 = \underline{}$

G.

Division: Related Facts

Solve each problem. Draw a picture to help you find the answer if you need help.

$6 \div 2 =$ **3**

$6 \div 3 =$ **2**

1. $12 \div 3 =$ _____

   $12 \div 4 =$ _____

2. $15 \div 5 =$ _____

   $15 \div 3 =$ _____

3. $10 \div 5 =$ _____

   $10 \div 2 =$ _____

4. $16 \div 2 =$ _____

   $16 \div 8 =$ _____

5. $20 \div 4 =$ _____

   $20 \div 5 =$ _____

6. $24 \div 6 =$ _____

   $24 \div 4 =$ _____

7. $28 \div 4 =$ _____

   $28 \div 7 =$ _____

8. $36 \div 9 =$ _____

   $36 \div 4 =$ _____

9. $14 \div 7 =$ _____

   $14 \div 2 =$ _____

Division Facts

Solve each problem.

$$5\overset{8}{\overline{)40}}$$

1. $6\overline{)42}$

2. $3\overline{)27}$

3. $2\overline{)16}$

4. $7\overline{)49}$

5. $8\overline{)56}$

6. $4\overline{)16}$

7. $9\overline{)45}$

8. $10\overline{)90}$

9. $6\overline{)48}$

10. $7\overline{)56}$

11. $9\overline{)36}$

12. $5\overline{)30}$

13. $8\overline{)72}$

14. $9\overline{)63}$

15. $7\overline{)42}$

Division Problem Solving

Solve each problem. Show your work. Then, write the answer on the line.

1. David has 12 goldfish. He has 2 fish tanks.

   How many fish will be in each tank if he divides them evenly?

   _____

2. Debbie bought 8 new bracelets. She will wear the same number on each wrist.

   How many bracelets will she have on each wrist?

   _____

3. Sam's team scored 16 points during the game. They scored the same number of points in each quarter.

   How many points did they score in each quarter?

   _____

4. Nick has 15 trophies. He displays the same number on each of 3 shelves.

   How many trophies are on each shelf?

   _____

Division: Facts of 3, 4, 6, and 7

Solve each problem.

1. $15 \div 3 =$ _____

   $21 \div 3 =$ _____

   $27 \div 3 =$ _____

   $6 \div 3 =$ _____

   $12 \div 3 =$ _____

   $18 \div 3 =$ _____

   $24 \div 3 =$ _____

2. $16 \div 4 =$ _____

   $24 \div 4 =$ _____

   $32 \div 4 =$ _____

   $40 \div 4 =$ _____

   $12 \div 4 =$ _____

   $20 \div 4 =$ _____

   $28 \div 4 =$ _____

3. $54 \div 6 =$ _____

   $18 \div 6 =$ _____

   $48 \div 6 =$ _____

   $24 \div 6 =$ _____

   $60 \div 6 =$ _____

   $42 \div 6 =$ _____

   $36 \div 6 =$ _____

4. $28 \div 7 =$ _____

   $42 \div 7 =$ _____

   $70 \div 7 =$ _____

   $56 \div 7 =$ _____

   $21 \div 7 =$ _____

   $35 \div 7 =$ _____

   $49 \div 7 =$ _____

Multiplication and Division: Fact Families

Solve each problem.

$9 \times 3 =$ __27__

$3 \times 9 =$ __27__

$27 \div 9 =$ __3__

$27 \div 3 =$ __9__

1. $4 \times 7 =$ _____

$7 \times 4 =$ _____

$28 \div 7 =$ _____

$28 \div 4 =$ _____

2. $2 \times 8 =$ _____

$8 \times 2 =$ _____

$16 \div 8 =$ _____

$16 \div 2 =$ _____

3. $5 \times 6 =$ _____

$6 \times 5 =$ _____

$30 \div 6 =$ _____

$30 \div 5 =$ _____

4. $6 \times 9 =$ _____

$9 \times 6 =$ _____

$54 \div 9 =$ _____

$54 \div 6 =$ _____

5. $8 \times 7 =$ _____

$7 \times 8 =$ _____

$56 \div 7 =$ _____

$56 \div 8 =$ _____

6. $45 \div 9 =$ _____

$45 \div 5 =$ _____

$9 \times 5 =$ _____

$5 \times 9 =$ _____

7. $42 \div 6 =$ _____

$42 \div 7 =$ _____

$6 \times 7 =$ _____

$7 \times 6 =$ _____

8. $63 \div 7 =$ _____

$63 \div 9 =$ _____

$9 \times 7 =$ _____

$7 \times 9 =$ _____

9. $36 \div 9 =$ _____

$36 \div 4 =$ _____

$4 \times 9 =$ _____

$9 \times 4 =$ _____

Multiplication and Division

Solve each problem.

$$\begin{array}{r} 5 \\ \times\ 4 \\ \hline 20 \end{array}$$

1. $$\begin{array}{r} 4 \\ \times\ 6 \\ \hline \end{array}$$

2. $$\begin{array}{r} 9 \\ \times\ 7 \\ \hline \end{array}$$

3. $$\begin{array}{r} 7 \\ \times\ 3 \\ \hline \end{array}$$

4. $$\begin{array}{r} 6 \\ \times\ 5 \\ \hline \end{array}$$

5. $3\overline{)27}$

6. $7\overline{)28}$

7. $5\overline{)40}$

8. $8\overline{)64}$

9. $81 \div 9 =$ ____

10. $7 \times 5 =$ ____

11. $28 \div 4 =$ ____

12. $6 \times 7 =$ ____

13. $24 \div 6 =$ ____

14. $18 \div 3 =$ ____

15. $8 \times 3 =$ ____

16. $27 \div 9 =$ ____

17. $20 \div 5 =$ ____

18. $10 \times 6 =$ ____

19. $54 \div 6 =$ ____

20. $8 \times 8 =$ ____

Multiplication and Division

Solve each problem.

$3 \times \underline{\mathbf{9}} = 27$ 1. $7 \times \underline{\hspace{1cm}} = 42$ 2. $5 \times \underline{\hspace{1cm}} = 50$

3. $\underline{\hspace{1cm}} \times 7 = 49$ 4. $9 \times \underline{\hspace{1cm}} = 81$ 5. $4 \times \underline{\hspace{1cm}} = 28$

6. $\underline{\hspace{1cm}} \times 5 = 45$ 7. $\underline{\hspace{1cm}} \times 4 = 12$ 8. $\underline{\hspace{1cm}} \times 8 = 72$

9. $\underline{\hspace{1cm}} \times 8 = 64$ 10. $6 \times \underline{\hspace{1cm}} = 48$ 11. $\underline{\hspace{1cm}} \times 7 = 63$

12. $\begin{array}{r} 3 \\ \times\, 4 \\ \hline \end{array}$ 13. $\begin{array}{r} 2 \\ \times\, 3 \\ \hline \end{array}$ 14. $\begin{array}{r} 10 \\ \times\, 6 \\ \hline \end{array}$ 15. $\begin{array}{r} 4 \\ \times\, 2 \\ \hline \end{array}$ 16. $\begin{array}{r} 8 \\ \times\, 0 \\ \hline \end{array}$

17. $\begin{array}{r} 2 \\ \times\, 4 \\ \hline \end{array}$ 18. $\begin{array}{r} 3 \\ \times\, 3 \\ \hline \end{array}$ 19. $\begin{array}{r} 7 \\ \times\, 4 \\ \hline \end{array}$ 20. $\begin{array}{r} 10 \\ \times\, 9 \\ \hline \end{array}$ 21. $\begin{array}{r} 5 \\ \times\, 1 \\ \hline \end{array}$

Multiplying by Multiples of 10

Solve each problem.

25 × 30

Step 1: Multiply by the number in the ones place.

$$\begin{array}{r} 25 \\ \times\ 30 \\ \hline 0 \end{array}$$

Step 2: Multiply by the number in the tens place.

$$\begin{array}{r} 25 \\ \times\ 30 \\ \hline 750 \end{array}$$

1. $\begin{array}{r} 15 \\ \times\ 10 \\ \hline \end{array}$

2. $\begin{array}{r} 63 \\ \times\ 10 \\ \hline \end{array}$

3. $\begin{array}{r} 43 \\ \times\ 20 \\ \hline \end{array}$

4. $\begin{array}{r} 51 \\ \times\ 30 \\ \hline \end{array}$

5. $\begin{array}{r} 36 \\ \times\ 20 \\ \hline \end{array}$

6. $\begin{array}{r} 26 \\ \times\ 40 \\ \hline \end{array}$

7. $\begin{array}{r} 52 \\ \times\ 30 \\ \hline \end{array}$

8. $\begin{array}{r} 33 \\ \times\ 50 \\ \hline \end{array}$

9. $\begin{array}{r} 48 \\ \times\ 30 \\ \hline \end{array}$

Multiplication without Regrouping

Solve each problem.

<table>
<tr><td colspan="2" align="center">21 × 4</td></tr>
<tr><td>Step 1: Multiply by the number in the ones place.</td><td>Step 2: Multiply by the number in the tens place.</td></tr>
<tr><td align="center">21
× 4
———
4</td><td align="center">21
× 4
———
84</td></tr>
</table>

1. 23
    × 2

2. 31
    × 2

3. 44
    × 2

4. 81
    × 2

5. 13
    × 3

6. 23
    × 3

7. 91
    × 3

8. 72
    × 3

9. 51
    × 4

10. 72
    × 4

11. 90
    × 4

12. 42
    × 4

13. 41
    × 5

14. 30
    × 5

15. 90
    × 5

16. 71
    × 5

Multiplication with Regrouping

Solve each problem.

---

38 × 8

Step 1: Multiply by the number in the ones place. Regroup.

$$\begin{array}{r} \overset{6}{3}8 \\ \times\ 8 \\ \hline 4 \end{array}$$

Step 2: Multiply by the number in the tens place. Add the regrouped amount.

$$\begin{array}{r} \overset{6}{3}8 \\ \times\ 8 \\ \hline 304 \end{array}$$

---

1. $\begin{array}{r} 17 \\ \times\ 7 \\ \hline \end{array}$

2. $\begin{array}{r} 19 \\ \times\ 7 \\ \hline \end{array}$

3. $\begin{array}{r} 23 \\ \times\ 7 \\ \hline \end{array}$

4. $\begin{array}{r} 46 \\ \times\ 7 \\ \hline \end{array}$

5. $\begin{array}{r} 63 \\ \times\ 8 \\ \hline \end{array}$

6. $\begin{array}{r} 22 \\ \times\ 8 \\ \hline \end{array}$

7. $\begin{array}{r} 92 \\ \times\ 8 \\ \hline \end{array}$

8. $\begin{array}{r} 83 \\ \times\ 8 \\ \hline \end{array}$

9. $\begin{array}{r} 84 \\ \times\ 9 \\ \hline \end{array}$

10. $\begin{array}{r} 27 \\ \times\ 9 \\ \hline \end{array}$

11. $\begin{array}{r} 94 \\ \times\ 9 \\ \hline \end{array}$

12. $\begin{array}{r} 57 \\ \times\ 9 \\ \hline \end{array}$

13. $\begin{array}{r} 72 \\ \times\ 7 \\ \hline \end{array}$

14. $\begin{array}{r} 97 \\ \times\ 8 \\ \hline \end{array}$

15. $\begin{array}{r} 36 \\ \times\ 9 \\ \hline \end{array}$

16. $\begin{array}{r} 44 \\ \times\ 7 \\ \hline \end{array}$

Multiplication Practice

Solve each problem.

$$\begin{array}{r} 63 \\ \times\ 7 \\ \hline 441 \end{array}$$

1.
$$\begin{array}{r} 65 \\ \times\ 3 \\ \hline \end{array}$$

2.
$$\begin{array}{r} 69 \\ \times\ 5 \\ \hline \end{array}$$

3.
$$\begin{array}{r} 64 \\ \times\ 9 \\ \hline \end{array}$$

4.
$$\begin{array}{r} 67 \\ \times\ 7 \\ \hline \end{array}$$

5.
$$\begin{array}{r} 77 \\ \times\ 5 \\ \hline \end{array}$$

6.
$$\begin{array}{r} 71 \\ \times\ 9 \\ \hline \end{array}$$

7.
$$\begin{array}{r} 70 \\ \times\ 6 \\ \hline \end{array}$$

8.
$$\begin{array}{r} 75 \\ \times\ 8 \\ \hline \end{array}$$

9.
$$\begin{array}{r} 76 \\ \times\ 4 \\ \hline \end{array}$$

10.
$$\begin{array}{r} 82 \\ \times\ 7 \\ \hline \end{array}$$

11.
$$\begin{array}{r} 85 \\ \times\ 6 \\ \hline \end{array}$$

12.
$$\begin{array}{r} 89 \\ \times\ 3 \\ \hline \end{array}$$

13.
$$\begin{array}{r} 83 \\ \times\ 9 \\ \hline \end{array}$$

14.
$$\begin{array}{r} 88 \\ \times\ 5 \\ \hline \end{array}$$

15.
$$\begin{array}{r} 90 \\ \times\ 7 \\ \hline \end{array}$$

16.
$$\begin{array}{r} 92 \\ \times\ 9 \\ \hline \end{array}$$

17.
$$\begin{array}{r} 96 \\ \times\ 8 \\ \hline \end{array}$$

18.
$$\begin{array}{r} 95 \\ \times\ 6 \\ \hline \end{array}$$

19.
$$\begin{array}{r} 99 \\ \times\ 4 \\ \hline \end{array}$$

20.
$$\begin{array}{r} 62 \\ \times\ 8 \\ \hline \end{array}$$

21.
$$\begin{array}{r} 79 \\ \times\ 7 \\ \hline \end{array}$$

22.
$$\begin{array}{r} 86 \\ \times\ 7 \\ \hline \end{array}$$

23.
$$\begin{array}{r} 94 \\ \times\ 5 \\ \hline \end{array}$$

24.
$$\begin{array}{r} 39 \\ \times\ 8 \\ \hline \end{array}$$

Multiplication Problem Solving

Solve each problem. Show your work. Then, write the answer on the line.

1. Jim brought strawberries to school to share. He wants each student to get 3. There are 29 students.

   How many strawberries does he need?

   _____

2. Kara has 7 feet of ribbon. She knows that there are 12 inches in each foot.

   How many inches of ribbon does she have?

   _____

3. Tina rode her bike 11 miles each day for 6 days.

   How many miles did Tina ride altogether?

   _____

4. Jack read 7 books. Each book had 48 pages.

   How many pages did Jack read?

   _____

Multiplication Practice

Solve each problem.

$5 \times 3 \times 2 =$ __30__

1. $10 \times 2 \times 3 =$ _____

2. $2 \times 6 \times 1 =$ _____

3. $3 \times 2 \times 10 =$ _____

4. $4 \times 10 \times 1 =$ _____

5. $5 \times 2 \times 10 =$ _____

6. $7 \times 2 \times 2 =$ _____

7. $4 \times 2 \times 5 =$ _____

8. $4 \times 5 \times 2 =$ _____

9. $6 \times 3 \times 3 =$ _____

10. $3 \times 1 \times 6 =$ _____

11. $14 \times 3 \times 0 =$ _____

12. $6 \times 2 \times 3 =$ _____

13. $1 \times 6 \times 9 =$ _____

14. $3 \times 5 \times 2 =$ _____

15. $2 \times 5 \times 0 =$ _____

16. $4 \times 3 \times 3 =$ _____

17. $1 \times 7 \times 8 =$ _____

Dividing by Multiples of 10

Solve each problem.

$$30 \overline{)180} \quad 6$$

1. $20 \overline{)180}$

2. $40 \overline{)320}$

3. $60 \overline{)420}$

4. $70 \overline{)350}$

5. $30 \overline{)270}$

6. $50 \overline{)400}$

7. $90 \overline{)810}$

8. $80 \overline{)400}$

Division without Remainders

Solve each problem.

Step 1: Divide the tens digit by the divisor. Then, multiply the partial quotient by the divisor and subtract.

quotient → **3**
divisor → 2)76
      − 6
        1

Step 2: Bring down the ones digit with the difference.

$$\overset{3}{2\overline{)76}}$$
$$\underline{-6\downarrow}$$
$$16$$

Step 3: Divide the divisor into that number, multiply, and subtract.

$$\overset{38}{2\overline{)76}}$$
$$\underline{-6\downarrow}$$
$$16$$
$$\underline{-16}$$
$$0$$

1. 5)95

2. 4)88

3. 5)80

4. 3)72

5. 7)98

6. 5)75

7. 6)978

8. 7)938

9. 3)591

Division with Remainders

Solve each problem.

$$\begin{array}{r} 7 \text{ R1} \\ 4\overline{)29} \\ -28 \\ \hline 1 \end{array}$$

$\longleftarrow$ **4 × 7 = 28**

$\longleftarrow$ Subtract 28 from 29.
Because 28 is less than 29,
the remainder is 1.

1. $5\overline{)98}$ 2. $4\overline{)75}$ 3. $7\overline{)95}$

4. $3\overline{)70}$ 5. $3\overline{)80}$ 6. $5\overline{)57}$

7. $4\overline{)97}$ 8. $3\overline{)95}$ 9. $8\overline{)75}$

10. $4\overline{)86}$ 11. $5\overline{)64}$ 12. $6\overline{)91}$

Money: Counting Coins

Find each total. Write it on the line.

The amount that a coin is worth is called its **value**. To find the value of a group of coins, find the coin with the largest value. Then, add the coins with lesser values to that amount.

$$\left(50¢\right) + \left(25¢\right) + \left(10¢\right) + \left(5¢\right) + \left(5¢\right) + \left(1¢\right) + \left(1¢\right)$$

50¢   75¢   85¢   90¢   95¢   96¢   97¢

The total value of the coins is **97¢**.

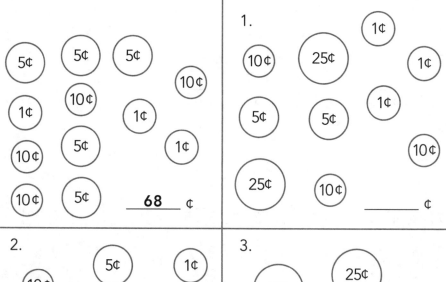

5¢   5¢   5¢

1¢   10¢   1¢   10¢

10¢   5¢   1¢

10¢   5¢   **68** ¢

1.

10¢   25¢   1¢   1¢

5¢   5¢   1¢

25¢   10¢   _____ ¢

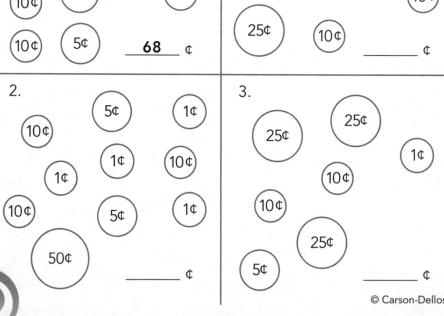

2.

10¢   5¢   1¢

1¢   1¢   10¢

10¢   5¢   1¢

50¢   _____ ¢

3.

25¢   25¢   1¢

10¢   10¢   25¢

10¢   5¢   _____ ¢

Money: Counting Money

Find each total. Write it on the line.

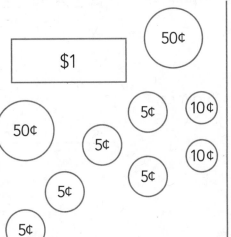

$1

50¢
50¢
5¢ 10¢
5¢
5¢ 10¢
5¢
5¢
5¢

$ __2.45__

1.

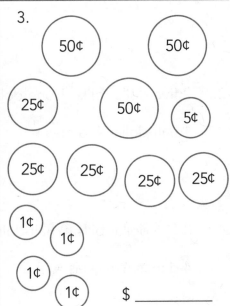

$5

$5

$5

50¢
10¢
10¢
10¢
25¢

$ _____

2.

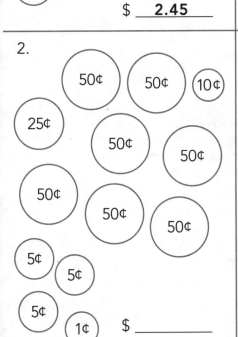

50¢ 50¢ 10¢
25¢
50¢
50¢
50¢
50¢
50¢
5¢
5¢
5¢
1¢

$ _____

3.

50¢ 50¢
25¢ 50¢
5¢
25¢ 25¢ 25¢ 25¢
1¢
1¢
1¢
1¢

$ _____

Money: Determining Totals

Find each total.

4 one-dollar bills, 3 quarters, 1 dime = $__**4.85**__

1. 5 one-dollar bills, 5 quarters, 5 dimes,

   15 pennies = $_____

2. 1 ten-dollar bill, 3 half-dollars,

   1 quarter, 7 nickels = $_____

3. 2 five-dollar bills, 1 one-dollar bill,

   1 half-dollar, 3 dimes = $_____

4. 3 five-dollar bills, 8 half-dollars,

   4 dimes, 9 nickels = $_____

Money: Addition and Subtraction with Regrouping

Solve each problem.

$735.41
+ 936.78
$1,672.19

1. $368.90
   + 657.85

2. $643.30
   − 286.53

3. $397.63
   + 583.97

4. $839.75
   − 659.75

5. $935.82
   − 758.97

6. $9,964.35
   − 797.66

7. $9,759.38
   − 7,788.68

8. $6,045.36
   + 3,587.88

9. $4,995.37
   + 9,327.83

10. $8,010.52
    − 7,936.67

11. $5,663.47
    + 5,459.53

12. $8,983.31
    − 5,975.86

13. $5,143.18
    + 8,867.92

14. $5,930.77
    − 5,688.33

Money Problem Solving

Four friends each have a different amount of pocket money to spend at Fun Night. Use the problem-solving matrix and the clues below to determine the amount of money that each person has.

- Joe has 3 pennies in his pocket.
- Kim has more than 13 quarters.
- Ty has only nickels and dimes in his pocket.
- Lily has only quarters in her pocket.

	$1.98	$4.03	$3.30	$1.75	$2.42
Joe					
Kim					
Ty					
Lily					

Money Problem Solving

Solve each problem. Show your work. Then, write the answer on the line.

Gina had $17.22. She earned $5.00 more for helping her mother.

How much money does Gina have now?

$17.22
+ 5.00
$22.22

1. Matt has $18.77. He wants to buy a DVD for $14.50.

How much money will he have left after he buys the DVD?

_____

2. Jon got $3.50 from his mother, $4.00 from his father, and $10.00 from his grandparents.

How much money did Jon get altogether?

_____

3. Len had $53.00. He is trying to earn enough money to buy a bike that costs $87.00.

How much more money does he need?

_____

4. Dan earned $20.00 for mowing a neighbor's yard. He already had $12.00.

How much money does he have now?

_____

5. Emma wants to buy a science kit that costs $18.00. She has only $6.00.

How much more money does she need?

_____

Equivalent Fractions

Use the pictures to find the equivalent fractions.

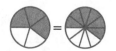 $\dfrac{1}{2}$ = $\dfrac{2}{4}$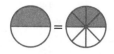

$$\dfrac{1}{2} = \dfrac{\mathbf{2}}{\mathbf{4}}$$

1. $\dfrac{3}{5} = \dfrac{}{10}$

2. $\dfrac{1}{2} = \dfrac{}{8}$

3. $\dfrac{2}{8} = \dfrac{}{4}$

4. $\dfrac{3}{9} = \dfrac{}{3}$

5. $\dfrac{1}{3} = \dfrac{}{9}$

6. $\dfrac{4}{8} = \dfrac{}{2}$

7. $\dfrac{4}{5} = \dfrac{}{10}$

8. $\dfrac{2}{3} = \dfrac{}{6}$

9. $\dfrac{6}{8} = \dfrac{}{4}$

Simplifying Fractions

Solve each problem.

To **simplify** a fraction, find the largest number that can divide evenly into both the numerator and the denominator.

For $\frac{3}{6}$, 3 can divide evenly into both 3 and 6, so $\frac{1}{2}$ is the simplest form for $\frac{3}{6}$.

$$\frac{3}{6} \div \frac{(3)}{(3)} = \frac{1}{2}$$

1. $\frac{4}{8} \div \frac{4}{4} = \underline{\quad}$

2. $\frac{4}{12} \div \frac{4}{4} = \underline{\quad}$

3. $\frac{5}{15} \div \frac{5}{5} = \underline{\quad}$

4. $\frac{4}{6} \div \frac{2}{2} = \underline{\quad}$

5. $\frac{2}{12} \div \underline{\quad} = \underline{\quad}$

6. $\frac{3}{9} \div \underline{\quad} = \underline{\quad}$

7. $\frac{3}{12} \div \underline{\quad} = \underline{\quad}$

8. $\frac{4}{16} \div \underline{\quad} = \underline{\quad}$

Adding and Subtracting Fractions

Solve each problem.

$$\frac{2}{5} + \frac{1}{5} = \frac{3}{5}$$

1. $\frac{3}{7} + \frac{2}{7} = $ ___

2. $\frac{5}{12} + \frac{6}{12} = $ ___

3. $\frac{4}{9} + \frac{3}{9} = $ ___

4. $\frac{3}{10} + \frac{6}{10} = $ ___

5. $\frac{5}{6} + \frac{1}{6} = $ ___

6. $\frac{4}{9} - \frac{2}{9} = $ ___

7. $\frac{7}{10} - \frac{2}{10} = $ ___

8. $\frac{7}{12} - \frac{3}{12} = $ ___

9. $\frac{7}{8} - \frac{6}{8} = $ ___

10. $\frac{4}{7} - \frac{1}{7} = $ ___

11. $\frac{4}{5} - \frac{2}{5} = $ ___

Fractions of a Set

Solve each problem.

Fractions can be used to describe parts of a set. Sometimes the sets are too large to draw pictures, so we can use division to help us.

Find $\frac{1}{4}$ of 28

$28 \div 4 = 7$

$\frac{1}{4}$ of 28 is **7**

$\frac{1}{3}$ of 21 = **7**

1. $\frac{1}{8}$ of 24 =

2. $\frac{1}{6}$ of 36 =

3. $\frac{1}{2}$ of 18 =

4. $\frac{1}{3}$ of 15 =

5. $\frac{1}{5}$ of 25 =

6. $\frac{1}{4}$ of 16 =

7. $\frac{1}{3}$ of 9 =

Fractions and Decimals: Tenths

For each picture, write the number of tenths, a fraction, and a decimal.

A **decimal** is a number that uses a **decimal point** (.) instead of a fraction to show tenths and hundredths.

A **tenth** is one out of 10 equal parts of a whole.

This picture can be written two ways.

1 tenth $\frac{1}{10}$ (fraction)

        0.1   (decimal)

1.

__1__ tenth

__$\frac{1}{10}$__ fraction

__0.1__ decimal

_____ tenths

_____ fraction

_____ decimal

2.

_____ tenths

_____ fraction

_____ decimal

3.

_____ tenths

_____ fraction

_____ decimal

Fractions and Decimals: Hundredths

Shade in the correct number of squares to match the decimal.

0.48

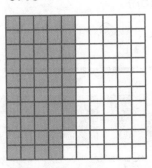

1. 0.73

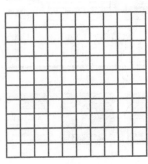

2. 0.31

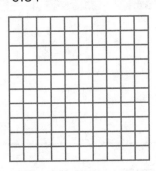

3. 0.17

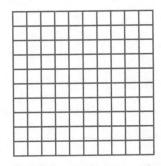

4. 0.69

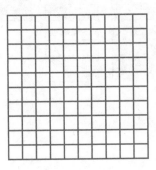

5. 0.24

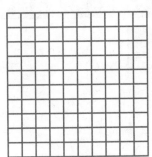

Decimals Greater Than One

Write the decimal to name each picture.

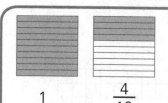 This picture can be written two ways.

$1\frac{4}{10}$ (fraction)

1 $\frac{4}{10}$ 1.4 (decimal)

1.

_____

2.

_____

3.

_____

4.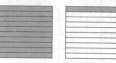

_____

Ordering Decimals

To order decimals with whole numbers like 1, 2, and 3, treat the whole numbers as decimals (for example, 1.0, 2.0, and 3.0). Then, compare the numbers as usual:

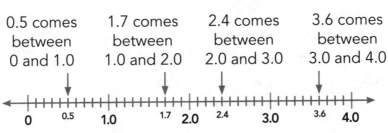

| 0.5 comes between 0 and 1.0 | 1.7 comes between 1.0 and 2.0 | 2.4 comes between 2.0 and 3.0 | 3.6 comes between 3.0 and 4.0 |

Write the missing decimals.

1.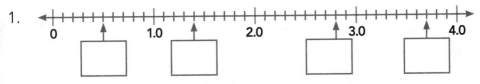

2.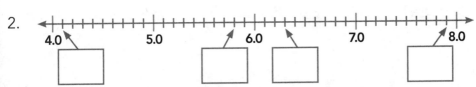

Write the decimals in order from least to greatest.

3.
0.1	1.6
0.7	1.3

⟶

4.
2.4	1.9
0.8	0.3

⟶

Adding and Subtracting Decimals

Solve each problem.

To add and subtract decimals, follow these steps:
1. Line up the decimal points.
2. Add or subtract the hundredths. Regroup if necessary.
3. Add or subtract the tenths. Regroup if necessary.
4. Add or subtract the ones.

$$
\begin{array}{r}
^12.4 \\
+\ 1.8 \\
\hline
\mathbf{4.2}
\end{array}
$$

1.
$$
\begin{array}{r}
6.7 \\
-\ 2.9 \\
\hline
\end{array}
$$

2.
$$
\begin{array}{r}
3.52 \\
+\ 0.78 \\
\hline
\end{array}
$$

3.
$$
\begin{array}{r}
2.6 \\
+\ 5.6 \\
\hline
\end{array}
$$

4.
$$
\begin{array}{r}
3.66 \\
-\ 0.48 \\
\hline
\end{array}
$$

5.
$$
\begin{array}{r}
9.59 \\
+\ 0.18 \\
\hline
\end{array}
$$

6.
$$
\begin{array}{r}
8.09 \\
+\ 1.36 \\
\hline
\end{array}
$$

7.
$$
\begin{array}{r}
7.3 \\
-\ 0.9 \\
\hline
\end{array}
$$

8.
$$
\begin{array}{r}
6.3 \\
-\ 4.8 \\
\hline
\end{array}
$$

9.
$$
\begin{array}{r}
1.8 \\
+\ 5.9 \\
\hline
\end{array}
$$

10.
$$
\begin{array}{r}
7.34 \\
-\ 2.16 \\
\hline
\end{array}
$$

11.
$$
\begin{array}{r}
6.03 \\
+\ 1.81 \\
\hline
\end{array}
$$

12.
$$
\begin{array}{r}
2.38 \\
-\ 0.16 \\
\hline
\end{array}
$$

13.
$$
\begin{array}{r}
4.99 \\
-\ 2.83 \\
\hline
\end{array}
$$

14.
$$
\begin{array}{r}
9.4 \\
-\ 0.7 \\
\hline
\end{array}
$$

15.
$$
\begin{array}{r}
3.7 \\
+\ 3.9 \\
\hline
\end{array}
$$

Measurement: Metric Units

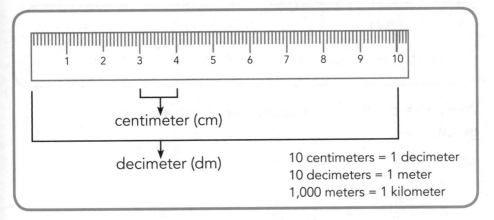

10 centimeters = 1 decimeter
10 decimeters = 1 meter
1,000 meters = 1 kilometer

Draw a line to connect the equivalent measures.

1. 4 km   40 cm

2. 40 m   4 m

3. 4 dm   4,000 m

4. 400 cm   400 dm

Circle the best unit to measure the item in each picture.

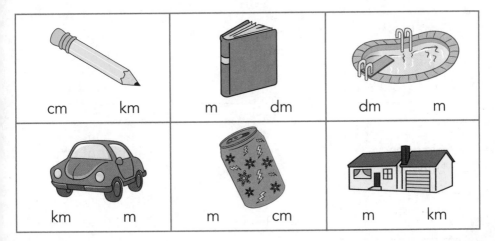

Measurement: Customary Units

| 12 inches (in.) = 1 foot (ft.) | 5,280 feet (ft.) = 1 mile (mi.) |
| 3 feet (ft.) = 1 yard (yd.) | 1,760 yards (yd.) = 1 mile (mi.) |

Write the equivalent measurement for each measurement given.

1. 6 ft. = _____ yd.

2. 48 in. = _____ ft.

3. 7 ft. = _____ in.

4. 4 yd. = _____ ft.

5. 36 in. = _____ yd.

Write the best unit to measure each item listed.

6. length of a driveway

_____

7. length of a camera

_____

8. length of a playground

_____

9. height of a door

_____

10. height of a table

_____

11. length of a book

_____

12. distance between two cities

_____

13. length of a swimming pool

_____

14. height of a person

_____

Polygons

Look at the figures. Answer each question.

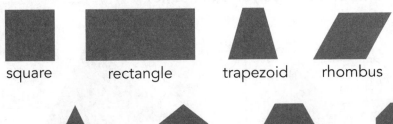

square   rectangle   trapezoid   rhombus   circle

triangle   pentagon   hexagon   octagon

1. What is the only figure with 4 equal sides and 4 right angles?

    _____

2. What figure has 3 sides and 3 angles? _____

3. What figure has no sides? _____

4. What figure has 5 sides? _____

5. What figure has 6 sides? _____

6. What figure has 8 sides? _____

7. Name four figures that have 1 or more pairs of parallel sides.

    _____   _____

    _____   _____

8. How is a trapezoid different from a rhombus? _____

    _____

    _____

Exploring Geometric Solids

Look at the geometric solids. Each side is called a face.
Write the number of faces for each solid.

1.

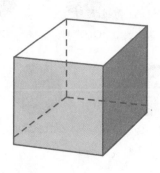

cube

_____ ☐ faces

2.

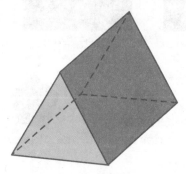

triangular prism

_____ △ faces

_____ ▭ faces

3.

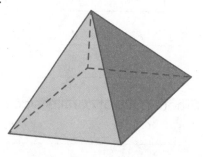

square pyramid

_____ ☐ face

_____ △ faces

4.

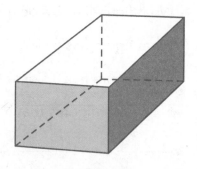

rectangular prism

_____ ▭ faces

_____ ▭ faces

Counting by 2s and 10s

Count by 2s and 10s.

1. Toes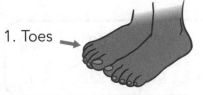

Did you count by 2s or 10s? ___

How many did you count? ___

2. Eyes

Did you count by 2s or 10s? ___

How many did you count? ___

3. Ears

Did you count by 2s or 10s? ___

How many did you count? ___

4. Fingers

Did you count by 2s or 10s? ___

How many did you count? ___

5. Elbows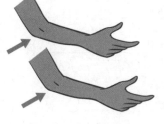

Did you count by 2s or 10s? ___

How many did you count? ___

6. Feet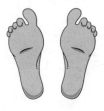

Did you count by 2s or 10s? ___

How many did you count? ___

Number Patterns

Write the next three numbers in each pattern. Complete the rule.

| 20 | 30 | 40 | **50** | **60** | **70** |

RULE: **Increase** the digit in the **tens** place by **1**.

1. 300   400   500   ____   ____   ____

RULE: _____ the digit in the _____ place by _____.

2.   5   10   15   ____   ____   ____

RULE: _____ the digit in the _____ place by _____.

3.   55   65   75   ____   ____   ____

RULE: _____ the digit in the _____ place by _____.

4. 700   600   500   ____   ____   ____

RULE: _____ the digit in the _____ place by _____.

5.   9   8   7   ____   ____   ____

RULE: _____ the digit in the _____ place by _____.

Data Analysis

Use the table to answer each question.

Eggs Laid by Insects or Spiders	
Insect or Spider	Number of Eggs
Water Spider	About 50–100
Cabbage Butterfly	About 300
Praying Mantis	About 10–400
Ladybug	About 3–300

1. Which insects or spiders can lay less than 150 eggs?

_____

2. What is the fewest number of eggs that the water spider lays?

_____

3. What is the greatest number of eggs that a ladybug can lay?

_____

4. Which insect can lay more than 300 eggs?

_____

5. If each insect and spider laid all the eggs possible, how many eggs would they lay altogether?

_____

Comparing Distances

The depth at which each of these ocean animals usually lives is given below.

Whale: 500 feet

Jellyfish: 10 feet

Shark: 250 feet

Octopus: 5,000 feet

Sponge: 300 feet

Crab: 1 foot

Lobster: 5 feet

Sea Bass: 100 feet

Suppose that you are in a submarine. Write, in order, the sea animals that you would see as your submarine dives to 5,000 feet.

1. _____

2. _____

3. _____

4. _____

5. _____

6. _____

7. _____

8. _____

Time Teaser

Draw a straight line to split the clock face below in half so that the sum of the numbers on one side of the line will equal the sum of the numbers on the other side.

Answer Key

Page 3
1. 5; 2. 10; 3. 7; 4. 10; 5. 9;
6. 5; 7. 11; 8. 19; 9. 5; 10. 6;
11. 17; 12. 13; 13. 0; 14. 12;
15. 8; 16. 12; 17. 3; 18. 15;
19. 9; 20. 15; 21. 7; 22. 7;
23. 12; 24. 4; 25. 9; 26. 14

Page 4
1. 10; 2. 10; 3. 13; 4. 10; 5. 13;
6. 10; 7. 9; 8. 14; 9. 9; 10. 7;
11. 7; 12. 9; 13. 13; 14. 5; 15. 6;
16. 8; 17. 16; 18. 7; 19. 9; 20. 15

Page 5
1. 13; 2. 13; 3. 11; 4. 15; 5. 17;
6. 13; 7. 15; 8. 15; 9. 18; 10. 18;
11. 16; 12. 17; 13. 17; 14. 18;
15. 18

Page 6
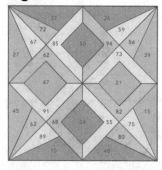

Page 7
1. 89; 2. 78; 3. 58; 4. 85;
5. 89; 6. 59; 7. 87; 8. 99;
9. 96; 10. 788; 11. 985;
12. 867; 13. 877; 14. 798;
15. 786; 16. 787

Page 8
1. 54; 2. 40; 3. 22; 4. 65; 5. 24;
6. 23; 7. 51; 8. 50; 9. 24; 10. 24;
11. 22; 12. 10; 13. 63; 14. 137;
15. 462; 16. 315

Page 9
1. 51; 2. 92; 3. 83; 4. 86; 5. 94;
6. 100; 7. 92; 8. 92; 9. 93;
10. 111; 11. 70; 12. 114; 13. 820;
14. 722; 15. 736; 16. 820

Page 10
1. 19; 2. 79; 3. 19; 4. 26; 5. 19;
6. 58; 7. 14; 8. 59; 9. 28; 10. 68;
11. 36; 12. 39; 13. 749; 14. 282;
15. 387; 16. 278

Page 11
1. 14 points; 2. 83 seashells;
3. 67 cars; 4. 81 bikes

Page 12
1. 158 cards; 2. 820 labels;
3. 640 rocks; 4. 257 fish

Page 13
1. 4, 9, 49; 2. 1, 5, 15; 3. 2, 0, 20

Page 14
1. 2, 1, 4, 214; 2. 2, 2, 7, 227;
3. 2, 8, 3, 283

Answer Key

Page 15
1. 1, 4, 6, 5, 0; 2. 0, 0, 0, 8, 1;
3. 4, 0, 7, 3, 6; 4. 0, 1, 4, 7, 5;
5. 5, 5, 8, 3, 7; 6. 8, 6, 9, 0, 2;
7. 0, 4, 5, 6, 0; 8. 3, 1, 0, 4, 8;
9. 0, 0, 1, 1, 1; 10. 7, 9, 2, 7, 7;
11. 0, 0, 0, 9, 3; 12. 9, 9, 9, 9, 9;
13. 0, 0, 0, 0, 5

Page 16
1. hundreds; 2. thousands;
3. ten thousands; 4. ten
thousands; 5. tens; 6. tens;
7. ten thousands; 8. hundreds;
9. thousands; 10. ones;
11. tens; 12. tens; 13. ones;
14. ten thousands;
15. thousands; 16. thousands;
17. hundreds; 18. tens;
19. thousands

Page 17
1. 75,947; 2. 93,755;
3. 157,479; 4. 569,121;
5. 340,312; 6. 253,506;
7. 716,098; 8. 628,201;
9. 926,035; 10. 147,430;
11. 671,356

Page 18
1. 148, 481, 184, 418; 2. 814,
841; 3. 184, 481, 418; 4. 814,
481; 5. 4,357; 4,375; 4,537;
4,573; 6. 5,437; 5,473; 5,734;
5,743; 7. 4,735; 4,753; 4,537;
4,573; 8. 3,547; 3,574; 3,745;
3,754

Page 19

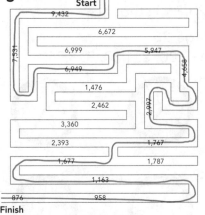

Follow the path in this order:
9,432; 7,531; 6,949; 5,947;
4,658; 2,997; 1,767; 1,677;
1,163; 958; 876.

Page 20
1. 6,712; 2. 9,809; 3. 6,308;
4. 9,046; 5. 8,180; 6. 8,066;
7. 6,195; 8. 5,191; 9. 6,906;
10. 7,600; 11. 7,424; 12. 5,008;
13. 9,087; 14. 6,041

Answer Key

Page 21
1. 1,296; 2. 2,067; 3. 4,728;
4. 6,035; 5. 3,760; 6. 3,559;
7. 5,032; 8. 4,802; 9. 1,909;
10. 2,063; 11. 1,879; 12. 3,696;
13. 4,086; 14. 1,274

Page 22
1a. 5,689 people; 1b. 731
people; 2a. 2,453 students;
2b. 195 students

Page 23
1. 6:00; 2. 1:30; 3. 3:55;
4. 5.

6. 7.

Page 24
1. 8:00, 7:40, 11:35, 9:05;
2. 1:35, 12:55, 6:55, 2:25;
3. 10:45, 6:30, 1:00, 12:00

Page 25
1. 2, 4, 8, 4, 2, 8; 2. 2, 6, 12, 6,
2, 12; 3. 3, 4, 12, 4, 3, 12; 4. 3,
5, 15, 5, 3, 15

Page 26
1. 12, 16; 2. 18, 21; 3. 12, 18;
4. 15, 20; 5. 28, 35; 6. 16, 20;
7. 27, 36; 8. 30, 36; 9. 16, 24;

Page 27
1. 3, 6, 9, 12, 15, 18, 21, 24, 27,
30; 2. 4, 8, 12, 16, 20, 24, 28,
32, 36, 40; 3. 5, 10, 15, 20, 25,
30, 35, 40, 45, 50; 4. 6, 12, 18,
24, 30, 36, 42, 48, 54, 60

Page 28
1. <; 2. >; 3. =; 4. <; 5. >; 6. >;
7. =; 8. >; 9. <; 10. <; 11. <;
12. =; 13. =; 14. >; 15. <; 16. <;
17. =; 18. <; 19. >

Page 29
1. $6 \times 9 = 54$ or $9 \times 6 = 54$;
54 marbles; 2. $4 \times 8 = 32$ or
$8 \times 4 = 32$; 32 cards;
3. $5 \times 9 = 45$ or $9 \times 5 = 45$;
45 times; 4. $7 \times 4 = 28$ or
$4 \times 7 = 28$; 28 skaters

Page 30
1. 7; 2. 7; 3. 8; 4. 8; 5. 6; 6. 9;
7. 9; 8. 6; 9. 5; 10. 20; 11. 12;
12. 0; 13. 4; 14. 7; 15. 7; 16. 4;
17. 5; 18. 0; 19. 7; 20. 10; 21. 9;
22. 5; 23. 10

Page 31
1. 30, 60, 54, 18, 42; 2. 48, 64,
40, 72, 56, 32; 3. 21, 28, 49, 42,
63, 35; 4. 45, 72, 27, 54, 81, 63

Answer Key

Page 32
1. 3, 3; 2. 5, 5; 3. 3, 3; 4. 4, 4;
5. 4, 4; 6. 2, 2; 7. 7, 7

Page 33
1. 6, C; 2. 7, A; 3. 5, F; 4. 8, G;
5. 3, D; 6. 9, E

Page 34
1. 4, 3; 2. 3, 5; 3. 2, 5; 4. 8, 2;
5. 5, 4; 6. 4, 6; 7. 7, 4; 8. 4, 9;
9. 2, 7

Page 35
1. 7; 2. 9; 3. 8; 4. 7; 5. 7; 6. 4;
7. 5; 8. 9; 9. 8; 10. 8; 11. 4; 12. 6;
13. 9; 14. 7; 15. 6

Page 36
1. 12 ÷ 2 = 6; 6 fish;
2. 8 ÷ 2 = 4; 4 bracelets;
3. 16 ÷4 = 4; 4 points;
4. 15 ÷ 3 = 5; 5 trophies

Page 37
1. 5, 7, 9, 2, 4, 6, 8; 2. 4, 6, 8,
10, 3, 5, 7; 3. 9, 3, 8, 4, 10, 7, 6;
4. 4, 6, 10, 8, 3, 5, 7

Page 38
1. 28, 28, 4, 7; 2. 16, 16, 2, 8;
3. 30, 30, 5, 6; 4. 54, 54, 6, 9;
5. 56, 56, 8, 7; 6. 5, 9, 45, 45;
7. 7, 6, 42, 42; 8. 9, 7, 63, 63;
9. 4, 9, 36, 36

Page 39
1. 24; 2. 63; 3. 21; 4. 30; 5. 9;
6. 4; 7. 8; 8. 8; 9. 9; 10. 35;
11. 7; 12. 42; 13. 4; 14. 6;
15. 24; 16. 3; 17. 4; 18. 60;
19. 9; 20. 64

Page 40
1. 6; 2. 10; 3. 7; 4. 9; 5. 7; 6. 9;
7. 3; 8. 9; 9. 8; 10. 8; 11. 9;
12. 12; 13. 6; 14. 60; 15. 8;
16. 0; 17. 8; 18. 9; 19. 28;
20. 90; 21. 5

Page 41
1. 150; 2. 630; 3. 860; 4. 1,530;
5. 720; 6. 1,040; 7. 1560;
8. 1,650; 9. 1,440

Page 42
1. 46; 2. 62; 3. 88; 4. 162; 5. 39;
6. 69; 7. 273; 8. 216; 9. 204;
10. 288; 11. 360; 12. 168;
13. 205; 14. 150; 15. 450;
16. 355

Page 43
1. 119; 2. 133; 3. 161; 4. 322;
5. 504; 6. 176; 7. 736; 8. 664;
9. 756; 10. 243; 11. 846; 12. 513;
13. 504; 14. 776; 15. 324;
16. 308

Answer Key

Page 44
1. 195; 2. 345; 3. 576; 4. 469;
5. 385; 6. 639; 7. 420; 8. 600;
9. 304; 10. 574; 11. 510; 12. 267;
13. 747; 14. 440; 15. 630;
16. 828; 17. 768; 18. 570;
19. 396; 20. 496; 21. 553;
22. 602; 23. 470; 24. 312

Page 45
1. 87 strawberries; 2. 84 inches;
3. 66 miles; 4. 336 pages

Page 46
1. 60; 2. 12; 3. 60; 4. 40; 5. 100;
6. 28; 7. 40; 8. 40; 9. 54; 10. 18;
11. 0; 12. 36; 13. 54; 14. 30;
15. 0; 16. 36; 17. 56

Page 47
1. 9; 2. 8; 3. 7; 4. 5; 5. 9; 6. 8;
7. 9; 8. 5

Page 48
1. 19; 2. 22; 3. 16; 4. 24; 5. 14;
6. 15; 7. 163; 8. 134; 9. 197

Page 49
1. 19 R3; 2. 18 R3; 3. 13 R4;
4. 23 R1; 5. 26 R2; 6. 11 R2;
7. 24 R1; 8. 31 R2; 9. 9 R3;
10. 21 R2; 11. 12 R4; 12. 15 R1

Page 50
1. 93; 2. 94; 3. 101

Page 51
1. 15.95; 2. 4.01; 3. 2.84

Page 52
1. 6.90; 2. 12.10; 3. 11.80;
4. 19.85

Page 53
1. $1,026.75; 2. $356.77;
3. $981.60; 4. $180.00;
5. $176.85; 6. $9,166.69;
7. $1,970.70; 8. $9,633.24;
9. $14,323.20; 10. $73.85;
11. $11,123.00; 12. $3,007.45;
13. $14,011.10; 14. $242.44

Page 54
Joe: $1.98; Kim: $4.03;
Ty: $3.30; Lily: $1.75

Page 55
1. $4.27; 2. $17.50; 3. $34.00;
4. $32.00; 5. $12.00

Page 56
1. 6; 2. 4; 3. 1; 4. 1; 5. 3; 6. 1;
7. 8; 8. 4; 9. 3

Page 57
1. $\frac{1}{2}$; 2. $\frac{1}{3}$; 3. $\frac{1}{3}$; 4. $\frac{2}{3}$; 5. $\frac{2}{2}$, $\frac{1}{6}$;
6. $\frac{3}{3}$, $\frac{1}{3}$; 7. $\frac{3}{3}$, $\frac{1}{4}$; 8. $\frac{4}{4}$, $\frac{1}{4}$

Page 58
1. $\frac{5}{7}$; 2. $\frac{11}{12}$; 3. $\frac{7}{9}$; 4. $\frac{9}{10}$; 5. $\frac{6}{6}$;
6. $\frac{2}{9}$; 7. $\frac{5}{10}$; 8. $\frac{4}{12}$; 9. $\frac{1}{8}$; 10. $\frac{3}{7}$;
11. $\frac{2}{5}$

Page 59
1. 3; 2. 6; 3. 9; 4. 5; 5. 5; 6. 4;
7. 3

Answer Key

Page 60
1. 5, $\frac{5}{10}$, 0.5; 2. 4, $\frac{4}{10}$, 0.4;
3. 9, $\frac{9}{10}$, 0.9

Page 61

1.

2. 　3.

4. 　5.

Page 62
1. 2.3; 2. 5.7; 3. 3.4; 4. 4.1

Page 63
1. 0.5, 1.4, 2.8, 3.7; 2. 4.1, 5.8, 6.3, 7.9; 3. 0.1, 0.7, 1.3, 1.6; 4. 0.3, 0.8, 1.9, 2.4

Page 64
1. 3.8; 2. 4.30; 3. 8.2; 4. 3.18; 5. 9.77; 6. 9.45; 7. 6.4; 8. 1.5; 9. 7.7; 10. 5.18; 11. 7.84; 12. 2.22; 13. 2.16; 14. 8.7; 15. 7.6

Page 65
1. 4 km = 4,000 m;
2. 40 m = 400 dm;
3. 4 dm = 40 cm;
4. 400 cm = 4m; pencil, cm; book, dm; pool, m; car, m; soda can, cm; house, m

Page 66
1. 2; 2. 4; 3. 84; 4. 12; 5. 1; 6. feet or yards; 7. inches; 8. yards; 9. feet; 10. feet; 11. inches; 12. miles; 13. feet or yards; 14. feet and/or inches

Page 67
1. square; 2. triangle; 3. circle; 4. pentagon; 5. hexagon; 6. octagon; 7. Answers may vary, but should include four of the following: square, rectangle, trapezoid, rhombus, hexagon, and octagon.; 8. The trapezoid has one pair of parallel sides; the rhombus has two pairs of parallel sides.

Page 68
1. 6; 2. 2, 3; 3. 1, 4; 4. 4, 2

Page 69
1. 10s, 10; 2. 2s, 2; 3. 2s, 2; 4. 10s, 10; 5. 2s, 2; 6. 2s, 2

Answer Key

Page 70

1. Increase, hundreds, 1;
2. Increase, ones, 5; 3. Increase, tens, 1; 4. Decrease, hundreds, 1; 5. Decrease, ones, 1

Page 71

1. water spider, praying mantis, ladybug; 2. about 50;
3. about 300; 4. praying mantis; 5. 100 + 300 + 400 + 300 = 1,100 eggs

Page 72

1. crab; 2. lobster; 3. jellyfish; 4. sea bass; 5. shark; 6. sponge; 7. whale; 8. octopus

Page 73

The sum of the numbers above the line is 39. The sum of the numbers below the line is 39.